CHRIST BIOGRAPHY FOR KIDS

The Story of a Little Athlete Who Never Gives Up!

Georgina G. Kerr

ONCE UPON A TIME, ON JUNE 7, 1996, A LITTLE BOY NAMED CHRISTIAN MCCAFFREY WAS BORN IN CASTLE ROCK, COLORADO.

As Christian grew up, he wasn't just any kid who liked to play outside

But Christian isn't just about football. Off the field, he loves playing the piano, spending time with his family, and helping others.

Copyright©Georgina G.Kerr
2024

All Rights reserved .No part of this publication may be reproduced,redistributed or transmitted in any form or by any means including photocopying ,recording ,or other electronic or mechanical methods without the prior permission of the publisher ,expect in the case of brief quotations embodied in critical reviews and certain other non commercial uses permitted by copyright law.

TABLE OF CONTENTS

CHAPTER 1:Who is Christian McCaffrey? 6
CHAPTER 2:Family of Athletes 6
CHAPTER 3:Young Christian's Dreams 6
CHAPTER 4:High School Star 6
CHAPTER 5:Stanford University Success 6
CHAPTER 6:The NFL Draft 6
CHAPTER 7:Rising Star in the NFL 6
CHAPTER 8:Christian's Super Skills 6
CHAPTER 9:Challenges Along the Way 6
CHAPTER 10:Joining the San Francisco 49ers 6
CHAPTER 11:Off the Field What Does Christian Love to Do Outside Football? 6
CHAPTER 12:Words of Wisdom from Christian 6
CHAPTER 13:QUIZ TIME! 6
CONCLUSION 6
GLOSSARY 6
The Silly and Fun History of How Football Started! 1

The Silly and Fun History of How Football Started!

A long, long time ago, before there were fancy football stadiums or cool jerseys, people were kicking around...wait for it...big round balls made of pig bladders! Eww! Yes, that's right—way back in history, people didn't have shiny, perfect footballs like we have today. They used whatever they could find, and sometimes, that meant kicking around things that were a little strange!

A Bunch of Ancient Kicks!

It all began in different places at the same time! Ancient people loved playing with balls. In China, there was a game called "Cuju" where soldiers kicked a ball to stay fit. Imagine kicking a ball while wearing armor—talk about toughness! Then over in Greece and Rome, people played a game called "Harpastum." But this game was wild! It was more about wrestling and tackling than kicking the ball—kind of like football mixed with wrestling. Sounds like a mess, right?

Medieval Football: Crazy Times!

Fast forward to the Middle Ages, and things got even crazier! In towns all across Europe, people played "Mob Football." This game had only one rule: GET THE BALL TO THE OTHER SIDE. No referees, no boundaries, and no time limits. It was a massive free-for-all! People would chase the ball down streets, through fields, and even knock each other over. It wasn't just kids playing—everyone was involved. The ball could be kicked, thrown, or carried...basically, anything went!

Kings and queens didn't like the chaos and tried to ban it, but football was too much fun, so people kept playing secretly. Shhh!

The Birth of "Proper" Football

Now, here comes the real twist! In the 1800s, schools in England decided, "Hey, maybe we should make some actual rules so people don't run into houses with the ball." At one school, Rugby School, some students liked picking up the ball and running with it, and that's how rugby was born. But at other schools, they preferred kicking the ball, and that's where the game we know as football (or soccer, in some places) came from.

By the year 1863, some smart people formed the Football Association and created the first set of official football rules! No more wrestling, no more crazy pig bladders, just kicking, passing, and scoring goals. Football was becoming a beautiful game!

America Adds a Twist

But wait, there's more! Over in America, people were like, "Why don't we combine football and rugby?" And voilà, American football was born! They added helmets, pads, and touchdowns, and the rest is history!

The Fun Never Ends!

And that's how football, in all its forms, got started! From ancient times of kicking weird balls to today's high-tech stadiums, football has always been about fun, teamwork, and a little bit of craziness. So, next time you kick a ball, remember—you're playing a game that people have loved for thousands of years (and, luckily, with much better balls!).

Now, get out there and score some goals—just don't chase the ball down the street like in the old days!

CHAPTER 1: Who is Christian McCaffrey?

Once upon a time, on June 7, 1996, a little boy named Christian McCaffrey was born in Castle Rock, Colorado. But this wasn't just any baby—Christian was born into a family where everyone loved sports. It's like he had football in his blood from the start!

As Christian grew up, he wasn't just any kid who liked to play outside. He was super fast! Whether it was racing his brothers, playing soccer, or throwing a football, he was always running around like lightning. In fact, his parents had to remind him to slow down, but Christian had big dreams, and slowing down wasn't part of the plan.

His dad, Ed McCaffrey, was a famous football player in the NFL, and his mom, Lisa McCaffrey, was a super-fast soccer player. So, you could say sports ran in the family!

Christian watched his dad play football on TV and thought, "Wow! I want to be just like him someday!"

The Little Kid with Big Dreams

Even when he was just a kid, Christian knew he wanted to be a football star. He played football in his backyard with his brothers, and they pretended they were in the big leagues. Christian practiced every day, and his speed and skills got better and better. It was like he had rockets in his shoes!

In high school, Christian wasn't just good—he was amazing! He could run faster than anyone on the field, and his teammates loved how hard he worked. Soon, everyone was talking about Christian McCaffrey. He was like a football superhero, and colleges from all over the country wanted him on their team.

Becoming a College Star

Christian decided to play football at Stanford University, where he became even more famous. People would watch him zoom across the field, dodging defenders and scoring touchdowns. It was like magic! Christian didn't just play football—he owned the field.

He was so good that he set records and won awards. Christian's hard work, speed, and love for the game had taken him to the next level!

The NFL Dream Comes True

Then, in 2017, something amazing happened. Christian's dream came true when he was drafted into the NFL by the Carolina Panthers. He was now playing professional football just like his dad! And guess what? He became one of the best players in the league in no time. He could run, catch, and score touchdowns like no one else.

People couldn't stop cheering for Christian because he was unstoppable on the field. He could zig-zag past defenders, leap over them, and make big plays. It was like he was a real-life superhero!

More than a Football Star

But Christian isn't just about football. Off the field, he loves playing the piano, spending time with his family, and helping others. He's a role model for kids everywhere because he shows that with hard work, you can achieve anything you set your mind to!

Christian McCaffrey is fast, fearless, and one of the best football players around. He started as a little boy with big dreams, and today, he's living those dreams, inspiring kids all over the world to chase theirs, too!

Growing Up with Football in His Blood

Christian McCaffrey didn't just grow up like any other kid—he was born into a football-loving family! It's almost like football was a part of him from the very beginning. Imagine having a dad who was a superstar football player and a mom who was a speedy soccer star—pretty cool, right?

His dad, Ed McCaffrey, was a legend in the NFL, playing for the Denver Broncos and winning Super Bowls! Christian would watch his dad play, hearing the crowd roar as Ed caught big passes and scored touchdowns. He thought, "One day, I'm going to be just like him!"

But it wasn't just about football. Christian's mom, Lisa McCaffrey, was a top-notch athlete too! She played soccer in college and was super fast, just like Christian would be. It's no wonder that when Christian was a little kid, he was already zipping around like a rocket, kicking soccer balls and tossing footballs with his brothers.

Family Football Fun!

At home, it was always game time. Christian had three brothers—Max, Dylan, and Luke—and they all loved sports. The backyard turned into their football field, and every day, they'd race, tackle, and toss the football to each other. Christian always gave it his all, even though he was one of the youngest. He wanted to prove he was just as good, if not better!

His family was always there to support him. His dad taught him how to be tough on the field, while his mom taught him how to be quick and smart. With every game, every practice, Christian was learning from the best!

Dreams of Becoming a Star

While other kids might dream of becoming astronauts or superheroes, Christian's dream was clear from the start—he wanted to be a football star! He practiced and played, never giving up, and with his family cheering him on, he knew he could do anything.

Growing up in the McCaffrey house wasn't just about playing sports—it was about working hard and following your passion. And with football in his blood, Christian was ready to make his dreams come true!

CHAPTER 2: Family of Athletes

Christian's Sports-Loving Family

Imagine a house where sports are as common as cereal for breakfast—well, that's the McCaffrey family for you! Christian McCaffrey grew up in a home where everyone loved playing sports, and each day was a new adventure.

The Super Dad

First, meet Ed McCaffrey, Christian's dad. Ed wasn't just any dad—he was a football hero! He played for the Denver Broncos in the NFL and won Super Bowls. Picture Ed running down the field, catching passes, and scoring touchdowns while thousands of fans cheered. At home, Ed wasn't just a football star; he was also a fantastic coach for Christian and his brothers. He'd take them outside to practice their kicks, throws, and catches. The McCaffrey backyard was their own little football field, filled with laughter and a lot of running around!

The Amazing Mom

Then there's Lisa McCaffrey, Christian's mom, who was a sports superstar in her own right. Lisa played soccer and was super fast—like a cheetah on the field! She'd show Christian and his brothers how to dribble a soccer ball, and her amazing footwork was something to see. Lisa also loved cheering from the sidelines, holding up colorful signs and shouting, "Go, team!" Her energy and enthusiasm made every game feel like a big celebration.

The Playful Brothers

Christian's three brothers—Max, Dylan, and Luke—were his partners in crime. They weren't just brothers; they were teammates and rivals, all rolled into one. They played football, soccer, and any other sport they could think of. The backyard was their arena, and they'd challenge each other to races, tackle each other in games, and make up fun rules as they went along.

Max was the oldest and liked to be the leader of their games. He'd come up with creative plays and always tried to show off his cool moves. Dylan, the middle brother, was known for his incredible speed. He could outrun anyone in their family, even Christian! And then there was Luke, the youngest, who was always full of energy and never afraid to jump into the action, no matter how big the game got.

Family Sports Nights

Sports weren't just for practice. The McCaffreys had special family sports nights! Every Friday, they'd turn their living room into a mini stadium. They'd play video games, watch sports on TV, and cheer for their favorite teams. Ed and Lisa would share stories from their own sports days, and Christian and his brothers would soak it all up, dreaming of the day they'd make their own sports stories.

The Big Dreams

Christian's family was always dreaming big. They knew that with hard work and practice, anything was possible. Whether they were practicing in the backyard, cheering at games, or just talking about their favorite sports moments, the McCaffreys were all about encouraging each other and having fun.

So, every day at the McCaffrey house was an adventure, filled with sports, laughter, and love. Christian grew up surrounded by the excitement of football and soccer, with his family cheering him on every step of the way. It was the perfect recipe for creating a future football star, and with a family like his, the sky was the limit!

How His Dad and Mom Inspired Him to Be Great

Christian McCaffrey had something special that helped him become the amazing football player he is today—two awesome parents who always inspired him to be his best! His dad and mom weren't just regular parents. They were like superheroes in the world of sports, and they filled Christian's life with lessons, love, and lots of motivation.

Dad, The Football Legend

First, let's talk about Christian's dad, Ed McCaffrey. Now, Ed wasn't just any dad—he was a NFL football star who played for the Denver Broncos and won three Super

Bowls! Can you imagine watching your dad catch passes and score touchdowns in front of thousands of fans? Christian did, and it made him dream of being a football star too.

Ed didn't just teach Christian about football, though. He taught him about the things that really matter in sports, like hard work, never giving up, and staying humble. Christian saw how his dad practiced every day, even when things got tough. Ed would tell him, "If you work hard and believe in yourself, you can do anything!" Christian soaked up all of his dad's advice like a sponge, and whenever he played football, he remembered his dad's words.

Ed also spent time in the backyard with Christian and his brothers, showing them the same moves that helped him become a champion. He'd say, "Don't be afraid to fail; that's how you get better!" Christian practiced those moves over and over, knowing that with each try, he was getting closer to being great like his dad.

Mom, The Soccer Speedster

But it wasn't just Christian's dad who inspired him—his mom, Lisa McCaffrey, was a huge part of his journey too! Lisa was a super-fast soccer player who had her own moments of sports glory. She wasn't just quick on the field, though—Lisa had the heart of a champion.

Lisa taught Christian how important it was to be determined and to always give his best effort, no matter what. She would tell him stories about her soccer games, where she had to run faster, think quicker, and work harder than her opponents. "Speed is important, but having heart and passion is what makes you a true athlete," she'd say.

Christian learned that it wasn't just about winning games—it was about giving everything you had and playing with joy and passion.

Christian loved how his mom always encouraged him to have fun. Lisa would remind him that even when games were tough, he should never lose sight of why he loved sports in the first place—because it was fun! That joy helped Christian stay positive, even when things didn't go his way on the field.

The Perfect Team

Together, Ed and Lisa were the perfect team for Christian. Ed gave him the tools to be tough and focused, while Lisa reminded him to stay passionate and have fun. Christian looked up to both of them, and their lessons were like little pieces of a puzzle that made him the incredible athlete he is today.

Whenever Christian faced a challenge, he'd think about his dad's determination and his mom's encouragement, and it gave him the strength to keep going. They inspired him to work hard, be humble, and always chase his dreams. And most importantly, they showed him that with a little love and support, anything is possible.

Now, Christian is following in his parents' footsteps, becoming a role model himself, and inspiring kids everywhere to dream big, just like his mom and dad did for him!

CHAPTER 3: Young Christian's Dreams

First Steps in Sports – Football, Track, and More

Christian McCaffrey didn't just dive into football right away—he tried all sorts of sports when he was little, and each one helped him become the incredible athlete he is today. From racing around a track to catching footballs, Christian's journey in sports was full of excitement and fun!

Running Like the Wind: Track and Field

Before he became a football star, Christian spent a lot of time running, and boy, was he fast! His mom, Lisa, who was a super-speedy soccer player, always encouraged Christian to use his speed. She signed him up for track and field, where Christian raced against other kids. He loved the feeling of his feet pounding the ground as he zoomed down the track, trying to be the fastest.

In track, Christian learned something important—how to push his limits. He practiced running every day, working on his speed and stamina. He wanted to be the fastest in every race, and his hard work paid off! Christian didn't just run; he won. He sprinted his way to the front of the pack and brought home trophies for his incredible speed.

But track wasn't just about running. It taught Christian how to stay focused and believe in himself. Whether he was running sprints or longer races, Christian learned that you always have to keep going, even when you're tired. And that lesson would become super important later on when he was running with a football tucked under his arm!

Kicking Off Football Fun

Of course, football was always a big part of Christian's life. With his dad, Ed McCaffrey, being an NFL star, Christian couldn't wait to play football like him. His first steps in football came when he was really young. He'd play with his brothers in the backyard, tossing the ball and practicing their catches.

At a young age, Christian joined his first youth football team, and he was already showing how fast and skilled he could be. Even though he was smaller than some of the other kids, he used his speed and smarts to dodge and dash past defenders. His coaches saw how special he was from the start. Christian had the unique ability to see the field in ways other kids couldn't—he knew just where to run and when to cut. His first steps in football were filled with touchdowns, tackles, and lots of fun.

Christian also loved playing different positions. He wasn't just a runner—he tried catching passes, too, just like his dad did in the NFL. Christian became a wide receiver, running down the field to catch passes, and a running back, sprinting past defenders with the ball in hand. He was learning all the important skills that would help him later in his football career.

A Love for Basketball

Christian wasn't only fast and good with a football. He also tried his hand at basketball! He played hoops with his brothers, racing down the court and shooting baskets. Basketball taught him how to think quickly and move fast, two things that would help him a lot on the football field. Whether he was dribbling down the court or passing to a teammate, Christian loved the fast-paced action of basketball. It helped him improve his agility, and those quick moves came in handy when he had to juke defenders in football!

Trying It All: Soccer, Baseball, and More

Christian didn't stop at just football, track, and basketball. He tried all sorts of sports growing up, including soccer and baseball. Soccer helped him build his footwork skills—he learned how to move swiftly with the ball, which came in handy when he needed to dodge tackles in football. And baseball taught him how to stay focused and keep his eye on the ball—perfect for when he needed to catch passes on the football field.

Christian's early steps in all these sports helped him become the amazing all-around athlete he is today. Whether he was racing on the track, catching passes in football, or shooting baskets in basketball, every sport helped him grow stronger, faster, and smarter.

The Path to Greatness

With every sport he played, Christian's confidence grew. He knew that each step he took in sports was leading him toward something bigger. The lessons he learned from track, basketball, soccer, and football all came together to make him the unstoppable athlete he is today.

So, whether you're racing your friends, kicking a soccer ball, or catching a football, remember Christian's story.

His first steps in sports taught him that with hard work and a little bit of fun, you can chase your dreams—and catch them!

Christian's Childhood Goals

When Christian McCaffrey was just a little boy, he already had big dreams and exciting goals. Growing up in a sports-loving family, it didn't take long for Christian to set his sights high. His goals weren't just about winning games; they were about becoming the best version of himself, both on and off the field.

Dreaming of Football Stardom

From the moment Christian could hold a football, he knew he wanted to be a football star, just like his dad, Ed McCaffrey. Christian would watch his dad play in the NFL and dream of one day running onto the field with thousands of fans cheering for him. He'd imagine himself making incredible plays, scoring touchdowns, and leading his team to victory. One of his biggest childhood goals was to one day play in the NFL, just like his hero—his dad. Every day, Christian practiced in the backyard, working on his speed, agility, and catching skills. He wanted to be the kind of player who could do it all—run fast, catch the ball, and make game-changing plays. His goal wasn't just to be good; he wanted to be great.

Being the Fastest

Christian's speed was one of his greatest talents, and from a young age, he set a goal to be the fastest kid on the field. He loved the feeling of racing past his opponents, leaving them in the dust. Whether he was on the football field, the track, or playing soccer, Christian always aimed to be the quickest. He wanted to be the player that no one could catch!

He set small goals for himself, like running faster times in track and improving his sprinting during football games. Each time he beat his own record, it made him feel like he was getting closer to achieving his bigger dreams.

Being a Well-Rounded Athlete

Even though football was his favorite, Christian's childhood goal was to be a well-rounded athlete. He loved playing different sports, and he didn't want to limit himself to just one. He played soccer, basketball, baseball, and even ran track. His goal was to learn from each sport and use those lessons to become a better football player. For example, soccer helped him with footwork, basketball taught him quick thinking, and track made him faster.

Christian believed that by playing many sports, he'd become stronger, more agile, and more focused. His goal was to take all the skills he learned and combine them to be the best athlete he could be.

Making His Family Proud

More than anything, Christian wanted to make his family proud. His parents, Ed and Lisa McCaffrey, were his biggest supporters, and he set a goal to live up to their example. His dad had won Super Bowls, and his mom was a star athlete too, so Christian's goal was to carry on the family tradition of greatness in sports.

But Christian also knew that being great wasn't just about winning games. His parents taught him that it was about working hard, staying humble, and being kind to others.

One of Christian's biggest goals was to be the kind of person his family would be proud of—someone who gave his best effort, treated others with respect, and stayed grounded, no matter how successful he became.

Staying Focused and Having Fun

Christian's childhood goals weren't all about serious competition. He also set a goal to always have fun. No matter how hard he trained or how important the game was, Christian wanted to enjoy every moment. Whether he was playing in a championship game or just tossing a ball around with his brothers, his goal was to keep smiling and love the game. His parents always reminded him that having fun was the most important part of playing sports.

Growing Into a Leader

As Christian got older, one of his goals was to become a leader on and off the field. He didn't just want to be the best player; he wanted to be the teammate everyone looked up to. He wanted to help others, share what he'd learned, and encourage his teammates to give their best too. Whether he was leading by example with his hard work or cheering his teammates on from the sidelines, Christian's goal was to inspire those around him.

The Big Picture

Christian McCaffrey's childhood goals were more than just dreams—they were steps that helped him grow into the amazing football player and person he is today. With a heart full of passion, a family cheering him on, and big goals guiding him, Christian set his sights on greatness. And with every goal he accomplished, he was one step closer to making his football dreams come true!

CHAPTER 4: High School Star

Shining in High School Football

When Christian McCaffrey hit high school, he was ready to show everyone just how talented he was. His journey from a kid dreaming of football stardom to a high school star was filled with hard work, dedication, and some amazing moments on the field. Here's how Christian made a big splash in high school football!

Joining the Varsity Team

As a freshman at Castle Rock High School in Colorado, Christian wasted no time making an impression. Even though he was younger than most of the players, he quickly joined the varsity football team. It wasn't common for freshmen to play at such a high level, but Christian's skills were too impressive to ignore.

He had always dreamed of playing football at a high level, and now, that dream was coming true. Christian's speed, agility, and football IQ made him stand out. It was clear that he wasn't just another player—he was a phenom in the making!

Breaking Records

Christian's high school football career was like a highlight reel of amazing plays. He didn't just play; he dominated. He became known for his explosive speed and incredible athleticism. During his sophomore year, Christian set records that made people sit up and take notice.

One of his biggest achievements was breaking the record for the most touchdowns in a season. He scored so many touchdowns that it seemed like he was always in the end zone. His ability to make big plays in crucial moments earned him a reputation as one of the most exciting players to watch.

Leading the Team

Christian wasn't just a standout player; he was also a leader. As he got older, he took on more responsibility and became a captain of the team. Leading his high school team was a huge honor and a big part of Christian's development as a player.

He inspired his teammates with his hard work and positive attitude. Christian's leadership meant he was not only a star player but also a mentor and motivator. He encouraged his teammates, shared his tips and tricks, and led by example both on and off the field.

Winning Championships

One of Christian's biggest goals in high school was to win a state championship. He knew that achieving this goal would be a great way to cap off his incredible high school career. With his amazing talent and leadership, Christian helped his team reach the state finals.

In a thrilling game that had fans on the edge of their seats, Christian played a key role in leading his team to victory.

His performance in the championship game was spectacular—he scored multiple touchdowns and made crucial plays that sealed the win for his team. It was a victory that Christian and his teammates would remember forever.

Standing Out and Gaining Attention

Christian's performance in high school didn't go unnoticed. His incredible achievements and record-breaking plays caught the eyes of college scouts and football fans across the country. He earned numerous awards and accolades, including being named All-American and receiving a spot on many prestigious football watchlists.

He became one of the most talked-about high school football players, and his future in football looked incredibly bright. College coaches and sports analysts were excited to see what he would do next and eagerly awaited his transition to college football.

Balancing School and Sports

While shining on the football field, Christian also worked hard in the classroom. He knew that being a great student was just as important as being a great athlete. Balancing schoolwork with football practice was a challenge, but Christian managed to excel in both areas. His dedication to his studies and sports showed that he was not only talented but also incredibly disciplined.

The Journey to College Football

Christian McCaffrey's high school years were filled with remarkable achievements and unforgettable moments. He set records, led his team to victory, and inspired everyone around him. His success in high school set the stage for his next big challenge: college football. With a stellar high school career behind him, Christian was ready to take the next step toward achieving his dreams of becoming a professional football player.

Breaking Records and Grabbing Attention

Christian McCaffrey's high school football career was nothing short of spectacular. As he took the field, he didn't just play; he broke records and grabbed the attention of football fans and scouts everywhere. Here's how Christian became a record-breaker and a headline-maker during his high school years.

Shattering Records

From his first game as a freshman, Christian McCaffrey was a force to be reckoned with. His combination of speed, agility, and skill made him stand out on the field. It didn't take long for him to start breaking records and setting new standards for high school football.

One of his most impressive feats was setting the record for the most touchdowns in a single season. Christian seemed to have an uncanny ability to find the end zone. Whether he was running the ball, catching passes, or returning kicks, he was always a threat to score. Fans and coaches watched in awe as Christian scored touchdown after touchdown, quickly becoming one of the most exciting players in high school football.

Christian didn't stop at touchdowns. He also set records for the most rushing yards in a season and the most total yards from scrimmage. His ability to rack up yards on the ground and through the air was unmatched. It was clear that he was not just a great player but an extraordinary one.

The Attention He Deserved

Christian's record-breaking performances didn't go unnoticed. As he continued to dazzle on the field, he grabbed the attention of sports analysts, college scouts, and media outlets. His name started popping up in headlines, and he became a hot topic in the world of high school football.

Television stations and sports blogs began featuring highlights of Christian's incredible plays. People from all over the country were talking about this young athlete who seemed to do everything right. College football programs took notice, and Christian was soon receiving scholarship offers from some of the biggest universities in the nation. Christian's achievements earned him several prestigious awards. He was named to the All-American team and received numerous honors for his outstanding performance. He was also invited to play in all-star games, where he competed against other top high school players from across the country.

Setting an Example

Beyond breaking records and grabbing headlines, Christian McCaffrey became a role model for young athletes everywhere. His hard work, determination, and sportsmanship set an example for other kids who dreamed of playing football. Christian showed that with dedication and perseverance, you can achieve great things.

He often spoke to younger players about the importance of working hard, staying focused, and never giving up on their dreams. His story inspired many young athletes to push themselves and strive for greatness, just like he did.

Looking Ahead

As Christian's high school career came to a close, it was clear that he had made an indelible mark on the world of football. His record-breaking performances and the attention he received set the stage for his next adventure: college football. Christian was ready to take his game to the next level and continue chasing his dreams.

His high school achievements were more than just records; they were a testament to his talent, hard work, and love for the game. Christian McCaffrey's journey from a high school star to a college sensation was just beginning, and the football world eagerly awaited to see what he would do next.

CHAPTER 5: Stanford University Success

Christian's College Journey at Stanford

After an electrifying high school career, Christian McCaffrey took his talents to Stanford University. His time at Stanford was a new chapter filled with exciting challenges, incredible performances, and valuable lessons. Here's how Christian's college journey unfolded as he made a name for himself in the world of college football.

Arriving at Stanford

In 2015, Christian McCaffrey began his college career at Stanford with high expectations. Known for his impressive high school achievements, he entered Stanford with a reputation as one of the top young athletes in the country. The campus was abuzz with excitement as fans and coaches eagerly awaited to see how Christian would perform at the collegiate level.

His transition to college football came with its own set of challenges. The game was faster and more physical, and he had to adjust to a new playbook and a new team. But Christian's work ethic and determination shone through as he quickly adapted to the rigors of college football.

A Stellar Freshman Year

Christian's freshman year at Stanford was nothing short of spectacular. He made an immediate impact on the field, showcasing his incredible skills as both a running back and a receiver. His versatility was one of his greatest strengths, and he used it to become a key player for the Stanford Cardinal.

One of the highlights of his freshman year was his performance in the Pac-12 Championship Game. Christian was instrumental in leading Stanford to victory, scoring a touchdown and making several key plays. His standout performance helped him earn the title of Pac-12 Offensive Player of the Year.

Breaking Records Again

Christian McCaffrey's time at Stanford was marked by record-breaking performances. His sophomore year was particularly remarkable. He set the NCAA record for all-purpose yards in a season with over 3,800 yards, surpassing the previous record held by the legendary Barry Sanders.

Christian also set the record for the most rushing yards in a single season at Stanford, showcasing his incredible ability to both run and catch the ball. His performances on the field earned him numerous accolades and solidified his reputation as one of the best college football players of his era.

The Heisman Trophy Contender

Christian's outstanding performances did not go unnoticed by the football world. During his sophomore year, he was a finalist for the prestigious Heisman Trophy, which is awarded to the most outstanding college football player in the country. Although he did not win the Heisman, being a finalist was a huge honor and a testament to his incredible season.

Christian's achievements on the field, combined with his leadership and sportsmanship, made him a standout player and a fan favorite. His ability to make big plays in crucial moments earned him respect from teammates, coaches, and opponents alike.

Balancing Academics and Athletics

While Christian was busy making headlines on the football field, he was also committed to his academic studies. Balancing the demands of college football with coursework was no easy task, but Christian managed to excel in both areas. He understood the importance of education and worked hard to maintain good grades while pursuing his athletic goals.

Christian's dedication to his studies and his sport made him a well-rounded student-athlete. He often spoke about the importance of staying focused and managing time effectively, sharing his experiences with younger athletes and students.

Preparing for the NFL

As Christian's college career progressed, it became clear that he was ready for the next step. His incredible performances at Stanford had positioned him as one of the top prospects for the NFL Draft. Christian worked hard to prepare for this transition, focusing on training, improving his skills, and showcasing his abilities to NFL scouts.

His time at Stanford was a crucial period of growth and development. The experiences and lessons he learned on and off the field helped shape him into the player he would become in the professional league.

A Legacy at Stanford

Christian McCaffrey's college journey at Stanford was marked by remarkable achievements and unforgettable moments. From breaking records to earning accolades and maintaining his academic performance, Christian's time at Stanford was a testament to his hard work, talent, and determination.

His legacy at Stanford continues to inspire young athletes who dream of achieving greatness both in sports and academics. Christian's college career was a crucial step in his journey, setting the stage for his successful transition to the NFL and his continued pursuit of excellence in football.

The Amazing Plays That Made Christian McCaffrey a Star

Christian McCaffrey's time at Stanford was marked by a series of spectacular plays that not only showcased his incredible talent but also solidified his status as a football star. Here's a look at some of the most amazing moments from his college career that made him stand out on the field.

The 2015 Rose Bowl Performance

One of Christian McCaffrey's most memorable performances came in the 2015 Rose Bowl against the Iowa Hawkeyes. Christian was nothing short of spectacular, showing off his versatility and playmaking abilities. He scored three touchdowns and gained a total of 368 all-purpose yards, a record for the Rose Bowl. His dazzling performance was instrumental in Stanford's 45-16 victory and helped secure the Rose Bowl MVP award for him.

Breaking the Single-Season All-Purpose Yard Record Christian's sophomore season was a showcase of his extraordinary abilities. One of his standout moments was breaking the NCAA record for most all-purpose yards in a single season. He accumulated over 3,800 yards, surpassing the previous record held by Barry Sanders. His ability to excel in both rushing and receiving made this record-breaking feat all the more impressive.

The 2016 Pac-12 Championship Game

In the 2016 Pac-12 Championship Game against the USC Trojans, Christian McCaffrey demonstrated his game-changing abilities once again. He rushed for 207 yards and scored a touchdown, leading Stanford to a 41-22 victory. His performance was crucial in securing the Pac-12 title and highlighted his skill and determination on the big stage.

The Electrifying Run Against UCLA

Christian's game against the UCLA Bruins was another highlight of his college career. In this game, he made a stunning 96-yard touchdown run that left fans and commentators in awe. The run showcased his incredible speed and agility as he burst through UCLA's defense, evading tackles and sprinting down the field for a memorable touchdown.

The Game-Winning Play Against Oregon

In a thrilling matchup against the Oregon Ducks, Christian McCaffrey made a pivotal play that sealed the game for Stanford. With just a few minutes left on the clock, Christian made a game-winning touchdown run that demonstrated his strength and determination. His ability to perform under pressure was a key factor in Stanford's 38-36 victory over Oregon.

The Impressive Catch and Run Against Washington State

Christian McCaffrey was also known for his exceptional receiving skills. In a game against Washington State, he made a spectacular catch and run that showcased his hands and speed. Christian caught a pass from the quarterback, made a few defenders miss, and sprinted down the field for a long touchdown. This play was a perfect example of his playmaking ability and versatility.

The Versatile Playmaking

Throughout his college career, Christian was known for his ability to make incredible plays both as a running back and a receiver. His versatility allowed him to contribute in multiple ways, whether it was running the ball, catching passes, or returning kicks. His ability to excel in various roles made him a unique and valuable player for Stanford.

The Impact of His Plays

Christian McCaffrey's amazing plays at Stanford were more than just highlights; they were moments that defined his college career and showcased his incredible talent. Each play demonstrated his speed, agility, and football IQ, making him one of the most exciting players to watch in college football. His performances not only helped his team achieve success but also set the stage for his future in the NFL.

Christian's ability to make big plays in crucial moments earned him accolades and respect from fans, coaches, and scouts. His spectacular performances at Stanford left a lasting legacy and established him as one of the standout players of his generation.

CHAPTER 6: The NFL Draft

Getting Drafted by the Carolina Panthers!

After an incredible college career at Stanford, Christian McCaffrey was ready for the next big step in his football journey: the NFL. The moment arrived during the 2017 NFL Draft, and it was a milestone that would shape his professional career. Here's how Christian McCaffrey got drafted by the Carolina Panthers and started his journey in the NFL.

The Excitement of the NFL Draft

The NFL Draft is one of the most exciting times in football. It's when college players like Christian McCaffrey find out which professional team will give them a chance to play in the big leagues. For Christian, the draft was a moment filled with anticipation and excitement. He had worked hard throughout his college career and was eager to see where his football journey would take him next.

The Big Announcement

During the 2017 NFL Draft, Christian McCaffrey was one of the top prospects, and teams were eager to see which team would select him. As the draft progressed, fans and analysts watched closely to see where he would land. When the Carolina Panthers were on the clock with the 8th overall pick, there was a buzz of excitement.

With the 8th pick in the first round, the Carolina Panthers made their choice: they selected Christian McCaffrey! The announcement was met with cheers and applause, and Christian's family and friends celebrated the moment with him. It was a dream come true for Christian, who was thrilled to join the Panthers and start his NFL career.

Joining the Panthers

Christian McCaffrey's arrival with the Carolina Panthers marked the beginning of a new chapter in his football journey. He joined a team that was known for its competitive spirit and strong performances. As a rookie, Christian was excited to bring his skills and energy to the Panthers and make an impact on the field.

From the moment he stepped onto the field for his first practice, it was clear that Christian was ready to make a difference. His speed, agility, and versatility quickly became evident to his coaches and teammates. Christian was not just a running back; he was a dynamic playmaker who could contribute in many ways.

Making an Impact

Christian McCaffrey's rookie season with the Panthers was impressive. He made an immediate impact, showcasing his ability to run the ball effectively and catch passes out of the backfield. His versatility allowed him to be a key player for the Panthers, and he quickly became a fan favorite.

One of the highlights of his rookie season was his first career touchdown. It was a memorable moment that marked the beginning of many more to come. Christian's ability to make big plays and contribute in various roles made him a valuable asset to the team.

Embracing the NFL Challenge

Transitioning from college to the NFL was a big step, but Christian McCaffrey embraced the challenge with enthusiasm and determination. He worked hard to adapt to the speed and physicality of the professional game, and his dedication paid off. Christian's work ethic and positive attitude helped him succeed in his new role with the Panthers.

Building a Career with the Panthers

Christian McCaffrey's time with the Carolina Panthers has been marked by continued success and growth. He has become one of the standout players in the NFL, known for his incredible performances and ability to make plays in critical moments. His contributions to the Panthers have solidified his reputation as one of the league's top running backs.

A New Chapter Begins

Getting drafted by the Carolina Panthers was a pivotal moment in Christian McCaffrey's career. It marked the start of his journey in the NFL and set the stage for his continued success. With his talent, dedication, and passion for the game, Christian has made a lasting impact on the Panthers and has become a star in the professional football world.

Christian's journey from college standout to NFL star is a testament to his hard work and determination. His story continues to inspire young athletes and football fans everywhere, proving that with dedication and perseverance, dreams can come true.

Christian's Dream Comes True

Christian McCaffrey's journey from a young football enthusiast to an NFL star is a story of hard work, perseverance, and dreams coming true. His dream of playing professional football was realized in a way that few athletes ever experience. Here's how Christian's dream became a reality and the exciting moments that followed.

A Lifelong Dream Realized

From a young age, Christian McCaffrey dreamed of becoming a professional football player. He grew up watching games, playing with his family, and working tirelessly to hone his skills. His passion for the game and his dedication to becoming the best he could be were evident throughout his youth and college years.

When Christian was selected by the Carolina Panthers as the 8th overall pick in the 2017 NFL Draft, it was the culmination of a dream he had worked so hard to achieve. The moment was a milestone not only for Christian but for his family, friends, and supporters who had been with him every step of the way.

The First Day with the Panthers

Christian's first day as a Carolina Panther was filled with excitement and anticipation. He arrived at the team's facilities, ready to start a new chapter in his career. Meeting his new teammates, coaches, and staff, Christian was eager to get to work and contribute to the team's success.

The team welcomed him with open arms, recognizing his talent and the impact he could make on the field. Christian's enthusiasm and dedication quickly made him a valued member of the Panthers. His first practice and training sessions were a chance for him to showcase his skills and demonstrate why he was a top draft pick.

The NFL Debut

Christian McCaffrey's NFL debut was a highly anticipated event. As he stepped onto the field for his first professional game, he felt a mix of excitement and nervousness. Playing against other top athletes in the league was a new challenge, but Christian was ready.

In his debut game, Christian made an immediate impression. He contributed both as a running back and a receiver, showcasing his versatility and playmaking abilities. The energy and passion he brought to the game were evident, and fans quickly saw why he had been such a highly regarded prospect.

Achieving Milestones

Throughout his rookie season and beyond, Christian McCaffrey continued to achieve milestones and make his dream come true. He set several records and earned accolades for his performances. His ability to run, catch, and contribute in various roles made him a standout player. Christian's success on the field was a testament to his hard work and dedication. Each game was an opportunity for him to showcase his skills and contribute to his team's success. His performances earned him recognition and respect from fans, coaches, and fellow players.

Inspiring Others

Christian's journey from a young dreamer to an NFL star is an inspiring story for young athletes everywhere. His dedication, hard work, and perseverance show that dreams can come true with the right attitude and effort. Christian often speaks about the importance of following one's passion and working hard to achieve goals.

He also emphasizes the value of staying humble and giving back to the community. Christian's success is not only a result of his talent but also of his positive attitude and commitment to making a difference both on and off the field.

Living the Dream

Christian McCaffrey's dream of playing professional football has not only come true but has also been marked by incredible achievements and memorable moments. His journey from a young football enthusiast to an NFL star is a testament to the power of dreams and the rewards of hard work.

As Christian continues to excel in the NFL, he remains a role model for aspiring athletes and a source of inspiration for anyone who dares to dream big. His story is a reminder that with passion, determination, and perseverance, dreams can become a reality.

CHAPTER 7: Rising Star in the NFL

Christian's First Seasons in the NFL

Christian McCaffrey's initial seasons with the Carolina Panthers were filled with exciting moments, challenges, and impressive achievements. Here's a look at how Christian's professional career began and how he quickly made a name for himself in the NFL.

Rookie Season (2017)

Christian McCaffrey's rookie season was a thrilling introduction to the NFL. As the 8th overall pick in the 2017 Draft, expectations were high, and Christian was eager to prove himself.

Starting Strong:

Christian wasted no time showcasing his skills. In his debut game against the San Francisco 49ers, he made an immediate impact by catching a pass for a 1-yard touchdown. This was just the beginning of his promising career.

Versatility in Action:

Throughout the season, Christian demonstrated his versatility. He played as a running back, a receiver, and even returned kickoffs. His ability to contribute in multiple areas made him a valuable asset to the Panthers. By the end of the season, he had accumulated over 1,000 total yards (435 rushing and 651 receiving) and scored 7 touchdowns.

Second Season (2018)

Christian McCaffrey's second season in the NFL saw him continuing to develop and solidify his role as a key player for the Panthers.

Becoming the Lead Back:

In 2018, Christian took on a larger role in the Panthers' offense. With more opportunities to be the lead running back, he showed his ability to carry the ball effectively. He rushed for over 1,000 yards and scored 7 touchdowns.

A Record-Breaking Performance:

One of the standout moments of his second season was setting a new career high with 100-yard rushing games. Christian's consistent performance and ability to make big plays earned him recognition as one of the top running backs in the league.

Third Season (2019)

Christian McCaffrey's third season was a breakout year that would define his career and establish him as one of the NFL's premier players.

Historic Performance:

2019 was a historic year for Christian. He had an outstanding season, rushing for 1,387 yards and receiving 1,005 yards, making him the third player in NFL history to record over 1,000 rushing yards and 1,000 receiving yards in the same season. His incredible performance earned him Pro Bowl and First-Team All-Pro honors.

Amazing Plays:

Christian's 2019 season was filled with jaw-dropping plays. He scored a total of 19 touchdowns (15 rushing and 4 receiving), which led the NFL. His ability to make explosive plays and his consistent production on the field made him a fan favorite and a key player for the Panthers.

Fourth Season (2020)

In 2020, Christian McCaffrey's season was marked by both highs and lows.

Injuries and Challenges:

Unfortunately, Christian faced some injury challenges during the 2020 season. He missed several games due to injuries, which affected his ability to contribute consistently. Despite this, when he was on the field, he continued to show why he was one of the top running backs in the league.

Returning Strong:

Christian's determination and work ethic were evident as he worked hard to return to form. His resilience and dedication to getting back on the field showcased his commitment to the game and his team.

Early Career Impact

Christian McCaffrey's early seasons in the NFL demonstrated his exceptional talent and versatility. From his impressive rookie debut to his record-breaking performances, Christian quickly established himself as a key player for the Carolina Panthers. His ability to make significant contributions both as a runner and a receiver set him apart and earned him recognition as one of the league's top stars.

Christian's journey in the NFL has been marked by exciting moments and challenges. His determination and skill have made him a standout player and a role model for young athletes. As he continues to build on his success, Christian's early career remains a testament to his hard work and dedication to the sport.

Becoming One of the League's Top Players

Christian McCaffrey's journey from a promising rookie to one of the NFL's top players has been remarkable. His exceptional talent, dedication, and hard work have set him apart as one of the league's brightest stars. Here's how Christian McCaffrey made his mark and earned his place among the NFL's elite.

Outstanding Performance in 2019

Christian's 2019 season was a game-changer. He became one of the most dynamic players in the league, showcasing his versatility and playmaking abilities.

A Record-Breaking Year:

In 2019, Christian achieved a milestone that only a few players in NFL history have reached. He became the third player ever to record over 1,000 rushing yards and 1,000 receiving yards in a single season. With 1,387 rushing yards and 1,005 receiving yards, Christian's ability to excel both on the ground and through the air highlighted his unique skill set.

Scoring Machine:

Christian's knack for finding the end zone was evident as he scored a total of 19 touchdowns during the 2019 season. This impressive feat led the NFL in touchdown scoring and demonstrated his ability to make plays in crucial moments. His performance earned him Pro Bowl and First-

Team All-Pro honors, recognizing him as one of the top players in the league.

Versatility and Playmaking

Christian McCaffrey's versatility is a key reason why he has become one of the NFL's top players. His ability to contribute in various roles has made him invaluable to the Carolina Panthers.

Running and Receiving: Christian is not just a standout running back; he's also a top receiver. His ability to catch passes out of the backfield and make plays in space adds another dimension to his game. Whether running through defenses or making spectacular catches, Christian's versatility makes him a constant threat on the field.

Big Plays and Clutch Performances: Christian's ability to make big plays in critical moments has set him apart. From game-changing runs to crucial catches, he has shown time and again that he can perform under pressure. His clutch performances have earned him respect from teammates, coaches, and fans alike.

Dedication to Improvement

Christian's rise to the top of the NFL has been driven by his relentless dedication to improving his game. He is known for his strong work ethic and commitment to excellence.

Training and Preparation:

Christian spends countless hours training and preparing for each game. His dedication to conditioning, skill development, and studying game film helps him stay at the top of his game. His preparation ensures that he is ready to face any challenge on the field.

Leadership and Teamwork:

Beyond his individual achievements, Christian is also a leader on and off the field. His positive attitude, work ethic, and support for his teammates have made him a respected leader in the Panthers' locker room. His ability to inspire and motivate others contributes to the team's success.

Recognition and Awards

Christian McCaffrey's outstanding performances have not gone unnoticed. In addition to his Pro Bowl and First-Team All-Pro selections, he has received numerous accolades and recognition for his contributions to the game.

Accolades and Honors:

Christian's impressive performances have earned him a place among the league's top players. His achievements are a testament to his talent, hard work, and dedication. As he continues to excel, Christian's reputation as one of the NFL's best players only grows stronger.

A Bright Future

Christian McCaffrey's journey to becoming one of the NFL's top players is a story of talent, determination, and hard work. His remarkable performances, versatility, and dedication have established him as one of the league's elite players.

As Christian continues to build on his success, his future in the NFL looks incredibly bright. His impact on the field and his leadership qualities make him a valuable asset to the Carolina Panthers and a role model for young athletes everywhere. Christian McCaffrey's rise to the top of the NFL is a testament to his incredible talent and unwavering commitment to the game.

CHAPTER 8: Christian's Super Skills

What Makes Christian McCaffrey So Special on the Field

Christian McCaffrey is an amazing football player who stands out on the field for several exciting reasons. Let's discover what makes him so special and why he's one of the most thrilling players to watch!

1. Lightning-Fast Speed

Christian McCaffrey is like a superhero when it comes to speed! Imagine a race car zooming down the track—that's how fast Christian can run. Whether he's rushing the ball or catching a pass, he can outrun defenders and make big plays. His incredible speed helps him score amazing touchdowns and leave defenders in the dust!

2. Super Skills with the Football

Christian isn't just fast; he's also super skilled with the football. He can catch passes from anywhere on the field, just like a magician catching a flying ball. His hands are so quick and precise that he rarely drops a pass. When he has the ball, it's like he's dancing through the defense, making moves that are hard for anyone to stop.

3. Versatility—Doing It All!

Christian is known for his versatility, which means he can do many different things really well. He can run the ball, catch it, and even return kicks. Imagine a player who can play multiple positions on a team and excel at each one—that's Christian McCaffrey! His ability to switch between roles makes him a valuable player for his team.

4. Tough as Nails

Even though Christian looks like he's having fun out there, he's also very tough. He works hard, trains hard, and never gives up, even when the game gets challenging. When he gets tackled, he gets back up and keeps going, showing his determination and grit. His toughness inspires his teammates and shows everyone that hard work pays off.

5. Clever Moves and Tricks

Christian McCaffrey has a bag of tricks when he's on the field. He can dodge defenders with clever moves and quick spins, just like a player in a video game. His ability to change direction quickly helps him avoid tackles and keep running towards the end zone. His tricks make watching him play super exciting!

6. Team Spirit and Leadership

Christian is not just a fantastic player; he's also a great leader. He encourages his teammates, helps them improve, and always cheers them on. His positive attitude and teamwork make him a favorite among his friends and coaches. Being a good leader means supporting others and working together to win games.

7. Always Trying to Be Better

One of the best things about Christian is that he's always trying to get better. He practices hard, studies the game, and learns from each play. His dedication to improving makes him a top player and shows that with effort and determination, anyone can reach their goals.

Christian McCaffrey's Magic on the Field

Christian McCaffrey's speed, skills, versatility, toughness, clever moves, team spirit, and dedication make him truly special on the football field. He's like a superhero of football, using his amazing talents to entertain fans and inspire young players everywhere.

Watching Christian play is like watching a thrilling adventure unfold. He shows us that with passion, hard work, and a bit of magic, we can all achieve our dreams. So next time you see him on the field, remember that he's not just a football player—he's a star making every game an unforgettable experience!

Speed, Strength, and Smart Plays

Christian McCaffrey is a football superstar known for three amazing qualities: his incredible speed, his impressive strength, and his smart plays on the field. Let's dive into what makes these traits so special and how they help him shine in every game!

1. Lightning-Fast Speed

Christian's speed on the field is like a rocket taking off! When he gets the ball, he can sprint past defenders in the blink of an eye. Imagine a superhero dashing through obstacles—that's how fast Christian runs. His speed helps him make big gains and score exciting touchdowns. Whether he's racing down the sideline or dodging defenders, his lightning-fast legs make him a thrilling player to watch!

Example: In a game against the Houston Texans, Christian used his blazing speed to break free for a long touchdown run, leaving everyone watching in awe.

2. Powerful Strength

Christian McCaffrey isn't just fast; he's also incredibly strong. He combines his speed with powerful legs and upper body strength. This means he can push through tackles, break away from defenders, and keep moving forward even when he's hit. Imagine a strong, determined athlete who can power through any challenge—that's Christian!

Example: During a game against the Cleveland Browns, Christian used his strength to push through a tough tackle and keep running, showing off his powerful running skills.

3. Clever and Smart Plays

What makes Christian truly special is not just his physical skills but also his smart thinking on the field. He makes quick decisions and clever moves that surprise opponents and create big plays. Whether he's choosing the best path to run or making a perfect catch, Christian's smart plays help his team succeed.

Example: In a game against the Atlanta Falcons, Christian made a brilliant play by quickly catching a pass and then dodging several defenders to score a touchdown. His quick thinking and clever moves made the play look effortless.

Christian's Winning Combination

Christian McCaffrey's speed, strength, and smart plays make him a standout player in the NFL. His lightning-fast runs, powerful strength, and clever decisions on the field come together to create an exciting and dynamic playing style.

When you watch Christian play, you're seeing a perfect blend of athleticism and intelligence. His ability to combine these skills not only makes him a thrilling player to watch but also helps his team win games. Christian McCaffrey's amazing qualities show that being a top football player is all about using your strengths, making smart choices, and always giving your best.

CHAPTER 9: Challenges Along the Way

Injuries and Tough Moments

Even the best football players like Christian McCaffrey face challenges and tough moments, and it's all part of their incredible journey. Let's explore how Christian tackled these obstacles with bravery and determination!

Injuries Happen

Imagine you're playing your favorite game, and suddenly you trip and fall. That's kind of what happens to football players when they get injured. It can be a bit like getting a temporary setback in a video game, where you need to pause and reset before you can get back to the action.

Christian's Injuries:

Christian McCaffrey has faced a few bumps and bruises during his career. These injuries made it tough for him to play in some games. It's like when you're really excited to play a game but have to take a break because you need to heal.

For example, during the 2020 season, Christian had some tough luck with injuries. He had to miss several games because of a sore ankle and a strained shoulder. It was frustrating for him because he wanted to be out there helping his team win. But just like any champion, Christian didn't let this get him down.

Tough Moments

Every hero faces challenges, and Christian McCaffrey is no different. Tough moments are like tricky levels in a game that require extra effort and determination to overcome.

Missing Games:

When Christian couldn't play, it was tough for both him and his fans. He missed being on the field, making incredible plays, and scoring touchdowns. But instead of giving up, he used this time to focus on getting better. It's like when you're taking a break from a game to practice a new skill.

Recovery and Rehab:

To get back on track, Christian had to go through recovery and rehab. This is a bit like training in a game's practice mode to improve and prepare for the next level. He worked with doctors and trainers, doing special exercises to heal and get stronger. Christian's determination to return to his best form was like leveling up in a game, where every bit of practice makes him better.

Coming Back Stronger

Christian McCaffrey's comeback from injuries is one of the most inspiring parts of his story. Imagine a hero who takes a break but comes back with even more strength and skill—that's Christian!

Determination and Hard Work:

Christian didn't let his injuries stop him. He worked hard every day to recover, showing that being a great player means not just being on the field but also working hard off it. His perseverance is like a hero training to defeat the final boss in a game.

Returning to the Field:

When Christian was finally ready to play again, it was like hitting the reset button and diving back into the game. His return was met with excitement and cheers from fans, as everyone was thrilled to see him back in action. He came back with renewed energy and eagerness to play, making his return even more special.

The Hero's Journey

Christian McCaffrey's journey through injuries and tough moments is a big part of what makes him a true hero. Just like in your favorite stories or games, overcoming obstacles and continuing to fight for what you love shows real strength and courage.

Even when faced with challenges, Christian's dedication and positive attitude helped him bounce back stronger. His story teaches us that it's okay to face tough times, but with hard work, determination, and a positive spirit, we can overcome anything and come back better than ever.

So, the next time you face a challenge or tough moment, remember Christian McCaffrey's journey. Just like him, you can keep pushing forward and come out on top, turning every setback into a stepping stone towards your goals!

How Christian Stayed Strong and Bounced Back

Even though Christian McCaffrey faced some tough moments with injuries, he showed incredible strength and determination to bounce back. Here's how he stayed strong and came back better than ever!

1. Keeping a Positive Attitude

Christian McCaffrey is known for his optimistic outlook. When he was hurt, he didn't let frustration take over. Instead, he focused on staying positive and keeping a can-do attitude. Imagine you're playing a game and you hit a tricky level. Staying positive helps you stay motivated and ready to try again, and that's exactly what Christian did.

Example: Even when sidelined, Christian shared encouraging messages with his fans and teammates. His positive attitude helped lift everyone's spirits and kept him focused on his goal of getting back to playing.

2. Hard Work and Dedication

To get back on the field, Christian put in a lot of hard work. This meant following a special recovery plan with exercises and therapy to heal his injuries. It's like when you practice hard in a game to improve your skills. Christian's dedication to his recovery was like training for a big challenge, showing his commitment to returning stronger.

Example: Christian worked with physical therapists and trainers to rebuild his strength. He did exercises to strengthen his muscles and improve his flexibility, preparing his body to be at its best.

3. Support from Family and Friends

Christian's family and friends played a big role in helping him stay strong. They cheered him on and provided support during his recovery. Imagine having a team of friends cheering you on during a difficult level in a game. Their encouragement made Christian feel better and more determined to succeed.

Example: Christian's family, including his parents and siblings, offered constant support and encouragement. Their belief in him helped him stay motivated and focused on his comeback.

4. Setting Small Goals

To stay on track, Christian set small goals during his recovery. Instead of focusing on the big picture, he tackled smaller milestones, like improving his strength or completing a workout. This approach is like leveling up in a game, where you complete smaller challenges to reach the final goal.

Example: Christian set goals for each week, such as increasing his running distance or improving his agility. Each small achievement was a step closer to getting back on the field.

5. Learning and Adapting

During his recovery, Christian took the time to learn more about his body and how to take care of it. He adapted his training and recovery techniques to ensure he was getting the best results. This is like adjusting your strategy in a game based on what works best for you.

Example: Christian learned new techniques and exercises that helped speed up his recovery and prevent future injuries. His willingness to adapt and improve helped him return stronger.

6. Enjoying the Process

Christian made sure to enjoy the recovery process, finding joy in small victories along the way. He celebrated each milestone, no matter how small. It's like celebrating each win in a game, which makes the journey more fun and motivating.

Example: Christian celebrated when he reached key recovery milestones, like running a certain distance or completing a tough workout. These celebrations kept him excited and focused on his goals.

The Amazing Comeback

Christian McCaffrey's comeback from injuries is a story of strength, resilience, and determination. By staying positive, working hard, receiving support, setting goals, learning, and enjoying the process, he was able to overcome challenges and return to the field better than ever.

His journey teaches us that even when things get tough, we can stay strong and bounce back with hard work and a positive attitude. Christian McCaffrey's story is a reminder that setbacks are just opportunities to come back stronger and keep chasing our dreams.

CHAPTER 10: Joining the San Francisco 49ers

A New Chapter in Christian's NFL Journey

Christian McCaffrey's NFL journey has been full of exciting moments and incredible achievements. As he turned a page in his career, a new chapter unfolded, bringing fresh opportunities and thrilling challenges. Let's dive into this new phase and discover what makes it so special!

Joining a New Team

Christian McCaffrey started a new chapter in his NFL journey when he joined the San Francisco 49ers. It was like opening a new book in an exciting series. Christian was ready for new adventures and eager to bring his talents to a fresh team. Just like in a game where you explore new levels, joining the 49ers gave Christian a chance to showcase his skills in a different setting.

Example: When Christian joined the 49ers, he quickly became a key player. His versatility and playmaking ability added a new spark to the team's offense.

Making an Impact

From the moment Christian arrived with the 49ers, he made a huge impact. His incredible speed, strength, and smart plays were a perfect match for the team. It was like finding the final piece of a puzzle—Christian's addition helped complete the 49ers' game plan and brought new excitement to their games.

Example: In his first game with the 49ers, Christian made an impressive debut by scoring a touchdown and contributing to a big win. His performance showed fans and teammates just how valuable he was to the team.

Setting New Records

In this new chapter, Christian continued to break records and set new ones. Every game was a chance for him to achieve new milestones and show off his amazing skills. It was like leveling up in a video game, with each record adding to his impressive list of achievements.

Example: Christian set a record for the most rushing yards in a single game for the 49ers. His outstanding performance earned him praise and excitement from fans and teammates alike.

Building Strong Connections

A big part of Christian's new chapter was building strong connections with his teammates. As he settled into his new team, he developed great chemistry with the 49ers' players and coaches. Working together as a team was key to their success, and Christian's positive attitude and leadership helped strengthen these bonds.

Example: Christian spent time working with his new teammates during practice, developing plays, and sharing tips. His teamwork and enthusiasm helped create a supportive and dynamic atmosphere.

Facing New Challenges

Every new chapter comes with its own set of challenges, and Christian's journey with the 49ers was no exception.

He faced new opponents, adapted to different game strategies, and continued to work hard to stay at the top of his game. Overcoming these challenges made each victory even more rewarding.

Example: Facing off against tough teams, Christian used his skills and experience to help the 49ers secure important wins. Each challenge was an opportunity for him to shine and contribute to his team's success.

Inspiring Fans and Future Players

Christian's new chapter in the NFL inspired many fans and young players. His journey showed that with hard work, determination, and a positive attitude, anyone can achieve their dreams. Christian's story became a source of motivation for kids who looked up to him as a role model.

Example: Young football players admired Christian's dedication and skill. Many were inspired by his success and wanted to follow in his footsteps, dreaming of one day becoming stars in their own right.

The Exciting Road Ahead

Christian McCaffrey's new chapter with the San Francisco 49ers is an exciting part of his NFL journey. With his incredible talent, hard work, and positive attitude, he continues to make a big impact on the field and inspire others.

As he continues to play and achieve new milestones, fans can look forward to many more thrilling moments and accomplishments. Christian's story reminds us that every new chapter brings opportunities to grow, shine, and make a difference.

Bringing His Skills to a New Team

When Christian McCaffrey joined the San Francisco 49ers, it marked an exciting new chapter in his football journey. Let's explore how he brought his amazing skills to his new team and made a big splash!

A Fresh Start with New Opportunities

Joining the 49ers was like starting a new adventure in a game. Christian McCaffrey had the chance to showcase his incredible abilities on a new stage. He was eager to use his speed, strength, and smart plays to help his new team win games and reach new heights.

Example: Christian's arrival was highly anticipated, and fans were excited to see how he would fit into the 49ers' game plan. His energy and enthusiasm were contagious, bringing a new sense of excitement to the team.

Making an Instant Impact

From the very beginning, Christian McCaffrey made a noticeable impact. He quickly adapted to the 49ers' style of play, using his skills to contribute right away. His ability to run, catch, and make plays kept defenders on their toes and gave his team an edge.

Example: In his debut game with the 49ers, Christian showcased his versatility by scoring a touchdown and making several key plays. His performance demonstrated how valuable he was to the team and how quickly he could make a difference.

Teamwork and Chemistry

One of the most exciting parts of bringing Christian to the 49ers was how well he worked with his new teammates. Building strong connections with the other players was crucial for success. Christian's positive attitude and collaborative spirit helped him bond with the team, making them stronger together.

Example: Christian spent extra time working with his new teammates during practices, learning their playing styles and developing effective strategies. This teamwork helped the 49ers execute plays more smoothly and efficiently.

Learning the Playbook

Joining a new team means learning a new playbook, and Christian was up for the challenge. He worked hard to understand the 49ers' strategies and how he could fit into their plans. Mastering the playbook was like learning a new game's rules, and Christian's dedication made the process smoother.

Example: Christian studied the 49ers' playbook thoroughly and participated in team meetings to get up to speed. His commitment to learning the new plays allowed him to make smart decisions and contribute effectively during games.

Showcasing His Talents

Christian McCaffrey's unique talents were on full display as he brought his skills to the 49ers. His speed, agility, and ability to make big plays were exciting to watch and helped elevate the team's performance. Christian's contributions were like adding a star player to a winning team.

Example: Christian made several memorable plays, including a long touchdown run and a spectacular catch. His ability to make plays from anywhere on the field showcased why he was such a valuable addition to the 49ers.

Inspiring the Team and Fans

Christian McCaffrey's arrival inspired both his new teammates and the fans. His hard work, enthusiasm, and skill energized everyone and created a sense of optimism. Fans loved watching him play, and his teammates appreciated his dedication and leadership.

Example: Christian's exciting performances and positive attitude lifted the team's morale and boosted fan excitement. His success on the field encouraged everyone to believe in the 49ers' potential and look forward to more great games.

A Bright Future Ahead

Bringing Christian McCaffrey's skills to the San Francisco 49ers marked the beginning of a thrilling new chapter in his NFL journey. With his incredible talents, teamwork, and dedication, Christian is set to make a lasting impact and contribute to the team's success.

As he continues to play with the 49ers, fans can look forward to more exciting moments and remarkable achievements. Christian's journey shows that with passion, skill, and teamwork, new beginnings can lead to amazing adventures and accomplishments on the field.

CHAPTER 11: Off the Field

What Does Christian Love to Do Outside Football?

When Christian McCaffrey isn't on the football field, he has plenty of other hobbies and interests that keep him busy and happy. Let's take a look at some of the fun things Christian loves to do when he's not scoring touchdowns!

Music Lover

Christian McCaffrey loves music! When he's not training or playing football, you might find him strumming a guitar. He enjoys playing songs and even writes his own music sometimes. Music helps Christian relax and have fun, and it's a great way for him to express himself. Example: After a tough game or practice, Christian might pick up his guitar and play a few tunes to unwind. His love for music gives him a chance to be creative off the field.

Family Time

Family is super important to Christian. He loves spending time with his family, especially his brothers, parents, and girlfriend. Whether it's playing sports together or just hanging out at home, Christian cherishes the moments he shares with the people closest to him.

Example: Christian grew up in a sports-loving family, so they often bond over games, whether it's watching football or playing basketball in the backyard.

Helping Others

Christian is passionate about giving back to the community. He started his own foundation, the Christian McCaffrey Foundation, to help people in need, including military families and children facing challenges. He loves using his platform as a football star to make a difference and help those who are less fortunate.

Example: Christian spends time visiting hospitals, meeting with kids, and supporting charities that help people in need. His heart for helping others shows that he cares about more than just football—he wants to make the world a better place.

Outdoor Adventures

Christian also enjoys spending time in the great outdoors. Whether it's hiking, fishing, or exploring nature, he loves being outside and staying active. His love for adventure helps him stay balanced and refreshed, especially during the football offseason.

Example: On a sunny day, Christian might head out to the mountains for a hike or grab his fishing rod for a relaxing day by the lake. It's his way of enjoying nature and staying connected to the outdoors.

Staying Fit in Fun Ways

Even though Christian is an elite athlete, he likes to stay fit in fun and creative ways. He enjoys playing different sports like basketball or going for a run. For Christian, staying active is a way of life, and he finds joy in all kinds of physical activities.

Example: When Christian isn't on the football field, you might catch him shooting hoops with friends or doing yoga to stay flexible and strong. He loves finding new ways to challenge his body and keep improving.

Balancing Fun and Football

Christian McCaffrey's life isn't all about football—he loves music, family time, helping others, and enjoying outdoor adventures. By balancing fun hobbies with his football career, Christian stays happy, healthy, and ready to take on whatever challenges come his way.

His story shows that even though he's a football star, it's important to have other passions and interests that make life fun and exciting!

4o

You said:

Music, family time, and helping others.

ChatGPT said:

ChatGPT

Music, Family Time, and Helping Others

Christian McCaffrey's life off the football field is just as exciting as his time on it! When he's not running for touchdowns or catching passes, Christian loves to focus on three things that make him happy: music, family, and helping others. Let's dive into each one and see what makes them so special!

Music: Strumming to His Own Tune

Christian McCaffrey has a deep love for music. Whenever he has some free time, you might find him with a guitar in his hands, playing his favorite songs or even making up his own. Music is a way for Christian to relax, unwind, and be creative. It's something that makes him feel good after a tough game or practice.

Example: Imagine Christian sitting on his couch after a long day of training, playing a soft tune on his guitar. He says that music helps clear his mind and gives him a way to express himself when he's off the football field. Whether he's playing alone or jamming with friends, Christian's love for music is a big part of his life outside football. Who knows? Maybe one day he'll even perform on stage!

Family Time: Moments That Matter

For Christian, family comes first. He grew up in a close-knit, sports-loving family, and spending time with them is one of his favorite things to do. His dad, mom, and brothers have always been a huge support system, and they share a lot of fun moments together.

Whether it's playing basketball in the backyard, watching a game, or just having a family dinner, these moments mean the world to Christian. His family has always been there to cheer him on, and now he enjoys every chance he gets to relax and be with them.

Example: Christian's dad, Ed McCaffrey, was a football star too, and Christian learned a lot from watching him play. Now, they bond over sports and family time, whether it's sharing old football stories or just having fun. Christian's family taught him the importance of hard work, kindness, and staying humble, and those lessons help him on and off the field.

Helping Others: A Heart Full of Giving

Christian is not just a football star—he's also a kind-hearted person who loves giving back. He started the Christian McCaffrey Foundation, which helps people in need, especially military families, kids who are sick, and those going through tough times. Christian believes in using his success to help others, and he's always looking for ways to make a positive impact.

Example: Christian often visit hospitals to meet with kids who are facing serious illnesses. He brings smiles to their faces, encouraging them to stay strong and keep fighting. His foundation also provides resources and support for military veterans and their families.

For Christian, helping others is a way to show gratitude for all the blessings he's received in life. It's his way of saying, "I'm here for you," and making sure that those who need a little extra help get it.

The Balance of Passion and Purpose

Music, family time, and helping others are what make Christian McCaffrey's life feel full. These passions help him stay grounded and give him joy outside of football. Whether he's playing guitar, spending time with his loved ones, or making a difference in the lives of others, Christian is always finding ways to stay connected to what matters most.

Through his love of music, family, and giving back, Christian reminds us all that being a great person is just as important as being a great football player!

CHAPTER 12: Words of Wisdom from Christian

Christian's Advice for Young Athletes

Christian McCaffrey knows what it takes to be successful on and off the football field, and he loves sharing his wisdom with young athletes who dream of reaching the top. Whether you're just starting out in sports or aiming for big goals, Christian has some advice that can help you along the way!

1. Work Hard and Never Give Up

Christian believes that hard work is the key to success. No matter how talented you are, if you don't put in the effort, it's tough to reach your goals. When he was young, Christian would spend hours practicing, whether it was running, lifting weights, or sharpening his football skills. He knew that if he wanted to be great, he had to give it his all, every single day.

Example: "If you want to be the best," Christian says, "you have to practice like you're the best—even when no one is watching. Keep pushing yourself, even when it gets tough."

2. Believe in Yourself

Confidence is super important for any young athlete. Christian knows that there will be moments when things don't go as planned, but it's important to always believe in yourself. Even when he faced injuries or tough challenges, Christian stayed positive and kept working toward his goals.

Example: "There will be hard days," Christian says, "but always believe that you can bounce back and achieve anything you set your mind to. Confidence comes from knowing that you've worked hard and prepared for the moment."

3. Learn from Every Experience

Christian encourages young athletes to learn from every game, practice, or competition. Whether you win or lose, there's always something to take away. He believes that mistakes and challenges help you grow stronger, and the more you learn, the better you become.

Example: "If you make a mistake, don't get discouraged," Christian says. "Look at it as a chance to improve. Every experience teaches you something new, and that's how you keep getting better."

4. Take Care of Your Body

Christian knows that taking care of your body is essential for any athlete. Eating healthy, staying hydrated, and getting enough rest are just as important as practicing. Injuries can happen, but staying healthy and strong gives you the best chance to succeed.

Example: "Your body is like your greatest tool," Christian explains. "If you take care of it, it will take care of you on the field. Eat well, stretch, and listen to your body."

5. Have Fun and Enjoy the Journey

Above all, Christian believes that sports should be fun! He loves playing football because it brings him joy, and he wants young athletes to remember that having fun is the most important part. Whether you're winning championships or just playing with friends, enjoying the game will keep you motivated.

Example: "Never forget why you started playing in the first place," Christian says. "It's because you love the game! Always have fun, and the rest will follow."

A Winning Recipe for Success

Christian McCaffrey's advice for young athletes is simple: work hard, believe in yourself, learn from your experiences, take care of your body, and most importantly, have fun! These tips have helped him become one of the best players in the NFL, and they can help any young athlete chasing their dreams, too.

So whether you're on the field, the court, or the track, remember Christian's words—and keep reaching for the stars!

Staying Focused, Working Hard, and Never Giving Up!

Poop

Christian McCaffrey's journey to becoming a football superstar wasn't always easy, but three key things helped him along the way: staying focused, working hard, and never giving up. These are the ingredients to success, and Christian knows that young athletes can reach their dreams if they follow this advice.

Staying Focused

Christian learned early on that staying focused was important if he wanted to be great. With so many distractions, like video games or hanging out with friends, it's easy to lose sight of your goals. But Christian made sure he stayed on track. He set goals for himself and worked hard to stay committed, even when it was tempting to do other things.

Example: "When I was a kid, I loved playing with my friends, but I always made time to practice. Staying focused on your dreams is what makes them come true!"

Christian says that keeping your eyes on your goals, whether it's practicing more or doing well in school, is one of the best ways to succeed.

Working Hard

No one becomes a star athlete without putting in the work! Christian practiced for hours, whether it was running drills, lifting weights, or studying the game. He didn't become a top player by luck—he worked hard every single day to improve. For him, every moment was a chance to get better.

Example: "There are no shortcuts to success," Christian says. "You have to work harder than everyone else if you want to be the best."

Christian's message to young athletes is to always give 100%, whether it's during practice or a big game. Hard work is the key to getting better and achieving your dreams.

Never Giving Up

Christian faced challenges along the way, like injuries or tough losses, but he never gave up. Even when things didn't go his way, he kept pushing forward. Christian believes that perseverance is what sets great athletes apart.

It's easy to quit when things get tough, but the real champions are the ones who keep going, no matter what.

Example: "There will be days when it's hard, but that's when you have to dig deep and keep going," Christian says. "Never give up on yourself or your dreams."

For Christian, the tough moments made him stronger. He encourages young athletes to keep going, even when things seem impossible, because that's how champions are made.

The Recipe for Success

Christian McCaffrey's story shows that staying focused, working hard, and never giving up are the secrets to achieving great things. Whether you're just starting in sports or aiming to be the best, these three principles can help you reach your goals.

So, whenever you face a challenge, remember Christian's advice: keep your eyes on the prize, work harder than ever, and never, ever give up! Your dreams are worth it.

CHAPTER 13: QUIZ TIME!

Test Your Knowledge with Fun Questions About Christian McCaffrey!

Now that you've learned all about Christian McCaffrey, it's time to see how much you remember! Get ready to test your knowledge with these fun and exciting questions.

Don't worry if you don't get them all right—just have fun and see how much you know about this amazing football star!

1. Where was Christian McCaffrey born?

A) New York

B) Colorado

C) Texas

D) California

2. What sport did Christian's dad, Ed McCaffrey, play?

A) Basketball

B) Football

C) Baseball

D) Soccer

3. What is Christian's favorite instrument to play?

A) Piano

B) Drums

C) Guitar

D) Violin

4. Which college did Christian McCaffrey go to?

A) Stanford

B) Harvard

C) Clemson

D) Alabama

5. What team drafted Christian into the NFL?

A) Denver Broncos

B) San Francisco 49ers

C) Carolina Panthers

D) New England Patriots

6. What does Christian love to do in his free time?

A) Paint pictures

B) Ride bicycles

C) Play guitar and spend time with his family

D) Skateboard

7. Christian McCaffrey started playing football at a young age. What other sports did he play as a kid?

A) Track and basketball

B) Tennis and swimming

C) Hockey and soccer

D) Golf and karate

8. What foundation did Christian create to help others?

A) The Christian McCaffrey Helping Hands Foundation
B) The Christian McCaffrey Cares Foundation
C) The Christian McCaffrey Foundation
D) The Touchdown for Kids Foundation

9. How does Christian stay strong and come back from injuries?

A) He takes long vacations
B) He works hard, stays focused, and believes in himself
C) He quits football for a while
D) He changes his diet completely

10. What makes Christian McCaffrey special on the field?

A) His cooking skills
B) His ability to paint portraits
C) His speed, strength, and smart plays
D) His dancing skills

How Did You Do?

Check your answers below and see how well you know Christian McCaffrey!

Answers:
B) Colorado
B) Football

C) Guitar

A) Stanford

C) Carolina Panthers

C) Play guitar and spend time with his family

A) Track and basketball

C) The Christian McCaffrey Foundation

B) He works hard, stays focused, and believes in himself

C) His speed, strength, and smart plays

Great job! Whether you got them all right or just learned something new, you're now a Christian McCaffrey expert! Keep chasing your dreams, just like Christian!

Football Challenges, Puzzles, and Coloring Fun!

Are you ready for some fun activities? Get your game face on because it's time for some football-themed challenges, brain-teasing puzzles, and creative coloring pages! Whether you love football or just want to have some fun, there's something here for everyone. Let's get started!

Football Challenge: Design Your Dream Team! Imagine you're the coach of your very own football team! Who would you pick to be on your team? Write down the names of players you know, or create your own dream team with made-up names. Be sure to include:

1 Quarterback

2 Running backs

3 Wide receivers

2 Defensive players

1 Special player who can play any position!

Now, draw a picture of your team on the field, ready to play!

Puzzle Time: Football Word Search

Can you find all the football-related words hidden in the grid? Look carefully in every direction—up, down, and sideways.

Words to find:

TOUCHDOWN

RUNNING

KICKOFF

FIELD

QUARTERBACK

PASS

DEFENSE

TEAMWORK

COACH

VICTORY

Crossword Puzzle: Football Fun!

Complete this crossword puzzle by answering the questions below!

Across

The person who throws the ball on a football team. (_ _ _ _ _ _ _ _ _ _)

What you score when you reach the end zone. (_ _ _ _ _ _ _ _ _)

The player who runs fast to catch the ball. (_ _ _ _ _ _ _ _ _ _ _ _ _ _)

Down 2. What a player does to kick the ball to the other team. (_ _ _ _ _ _) 4. The team leader who helps players learn and practice. (_ _ _ _)

(Provide a blank crossword grid for kids to fill in.)

Create Your Own End Zone Dance!

After every touchdown, players celebrate with a fun dance. Now it's your turn! Think of your best dance moves and create a touchdown dance. You can:

Spin in a circle

Jump up high

Clap your hands

Or come up with something totally new!

Practice your dance and show it off to your family or friends! Who has the coolest touchdown dance?

CONCLUSION

Christian McCaffrey's football journey is nothing short of amazing! Born on June 7, 1996, in Colorado, Christian grew up in a family that loved sports. His dad, Ed McCaffrey, was a famous football player, and his mom, Lisa, was a talented soccer player. With such athletic parents, Christian was inspired to work hard and follow in their footsteps.

As a kid, Christian loved all kinds of sports—football, track, basketball, you name it! But football was where his heart truly belonged. He set big goals for himself and always gave his best, whether it was practicing or playing in games.

In high school, Christian became a football superstar, breaking records and grabbing everyone's attention. Colleges all over the country wanted him, but he chose to attend Stanford University, where he shines even brighter. His incredible plays made him a star, and soon, he was ready for the big leagues.

In 2017, Christian's dream came true when he was drafted by the Carolina Panthers in the NFL. His first seasons were filled with incredible performances, and it wasn't long before he became one of the top players in the league. Known for his speed, strength, and smart plays, Christian amazed fans and teammates alike.

But like any great athlete, Christian faced tough times too. Injuries slowed him down, but he never gave up. With hard work and determination, he bounced back stronger than ever, showing everyone what it means to be resilient. Now, as a star on a new team, Christian continues to shine on the field. Off the field, he enjoys playing music, spending time with family, and helping others through his charitable work.

Christian McCaffrey's journey shows that with hard work, focus, and a never-give-up attitude, you can achieve anything—even your biggest dreams!

GLOSSARY

Glossary for Christian McCaffrey's Story
Here are some important words and terms that will help you understand Christian McCaffrey's story even better. These are words related to football, sports, and Christian's amazing journey!

1. NFL (National Football League)

The professional football league in the United States where the best players in the country, including Christian McCaffrey, compete.

2. Draft

An event where professional teams choose players from college to join their teams. Christian was drafted by the Carolina Panthers in 2017.

3. Running Back

Christian McCaffrey's position on the football field. A running back is a player who runs with the football and tries to gain yards for the team.

4. Touchdown

A big play in football! It happens when a player carries the ball into the opponent's end zone. Christian is known for scoring many touchdowns!

5. End Zone

The area at each end of the football field. When a player reaches this area with the ball, it's a touchdown!

6. Offense

The team that has the football and is trying to score points by getting the ball into the end zone.

7. Defense

The team trying to stop the other team from scoring. They block, tackle, and try to get the ball back.

8. Training

Practice and exercises that athletes like Christian McCaffrey do to stay in top shape and improve their skills.

9. Injury

When a player gets hurt while playing sports. Christian had to deal with injuries during his career, but he worked hard to recover and play again.

10. Resilience

The ability to bounce back from tough times. Christian showed resilience by coming back strong after his injuries.

11. Stanford University

The college Christian attended, where he became a football star before joining the NFL.

12. Speed

How fast someone can move. Christian is famous for his incredible speed on the football field!

13. Strength

Christian is known for being strong, which helps him break tackles and push through defenders.

14. Teammates

The other players on Christian's football team work together to win games.

15. Coach
A person who teaches and trains the players, helping them improve and plan strategies for the game.

16. Foundation
A charitable organization. Christian created the Christian McCaffrey Foundation to help people in need and make a positive difference.

17. Huddle
When the players on a football team gather in a circle to discuss the next play.

18. Record
A performance that is the best of its kind. Christian broke several records in football, including the most yards gained in a season.

19. Focus
Concentrating on the task at hand. Christian says that staying focused is one of the keys to being great in sports.

20. Goal
Something you want to achieve. As a kid, Christian set goals for himself, like becoming a professional football player, and he worked hard to achieve them!

Made in the USA
Monee, IL
22 May 2025

17941123R00056